The King Has Spoken!

Ladies Can We Talk?

Author: Valerie D. Jones

The King Has Spoken!
Ladies Can We Talk?

Published by
DQ Spirit Works, LLC
P.O. Box 554
Dayton, OH 45404

Copyright © 2014 by Valerie D. Jones

All rights reserved.
No part of this book may be reproduced, stored in a retrieval system, or transmitted in any form or by any means — electronic, mechanical, photocopying, recording, or otherwise — without prior permission in writing from the copyright holder except provided by USA copyright law.

Scripture quotations are from the Kings James version (KJV) of THE HOLY BIBLE. THE KJV was published in 1611 and is public domain in the United States.

ISBN-13: 978-0-615-99035-4

Library of Congress Control Number: 2014935950

First American Paperback Edition

Printed in the United States of American

Table of Contents

7 Forward

9 Preface

11 ACKNOWLEDGEMENTS

15 About the Author

17 Introduction

19 *Chapter 1*
Where It All Began

29 *Chapter 2*
There is a Reason Why I'm Here!

35 *Chapter 3*
What Did I Do?

43 *Chapter 4*
Words, Words, and More Words!
This is What They Called Me

55 *Chapter 5*
How Do I Get Up From Here?

61 *Chapter 6*
What's Next ??

69 *Chapter 7*
Getting Started

Table of Contents

77 *Chapter 8*
Maintaining Your New Found Freedom

91 More Jewels of Wisdom

101 Testimonies
"BE ENCOURAGED"

> **103** I'm Victorious
> *Written by: Valerie D. Jones*
>
> **105** Biography of Ms. Shalonda Stroud
>
> **107** This Too Shall Pass
> *Written By: Ms. Shalonda Stroud*
>
> **115** "Where Do I Go"
> *Written by: Valerie D. Jones*
>
> **117** Biography of Ms. Stephanie D. Johnson-Chambers
>
> **119** Life after Divorce
> *Written by: Ms. Stephanie D. Chambers*
>
> **125** It's Knocking
> *Written by: Takelia V. Day*
>
> **127** Biography of Mrs. Takelia V. Day
>
> **129** Who Says I Can't Have it All?
> *Written by: Takelia V. Day*
>
> **135** From the heart of Valerie
> *Written by: Valerie D. Jones*

Forward

I believe after reading a chapter that this book will truly be an inspirational milestone to women all over the world. The way it explains to women of just how IMPORTANT women are to the survival of not only the family but the human race as well. It gives a clear view of the adversary's mission as it pertains to women and how the devil tries to hinder the love of a woman by any means he can. I was truly impressed as to how the chapter emphasizes that anytime women (or men) put anything before the WORD of GOD whether it be knowingly or unknowingly it can be a detriment to not only them but their family as well because it then becomes truth in their own mind.

I truly believe and feel that men as well as women will benefit from this book as it gives an insight to the minds of women we have chosen to live our lives with under the covering of God.

Steven Vestal
A Kingseye Photography

FORWARD

Interesting, Controversial, and an inspirational read. Makes a great book club discussion. I'm personally looking forward to reading more books by this author.

~Stephanie Jackson, CEO~
Tigress Lane Enterprises

God gave you a gift to touch many women around the world. I am so glad that I was chosen to be one of those women. As I finished the book I wanted more. Your book touched me in several chapters as I know it will do for others. Stay blessed!

~Shari Youmans~

Ladies Can We Talk is a spiritual recipe for transforming your self-esteem from a tiny fragile morsel into a heavenly gourmet four course meal. Through shared experiences you will discover the ingredients for creating the amazing "YOU" that God always intended from the beginning.

~Minister Stephanie Wilson Halfacre~
Inspirational Speaker and Author of
DreamQuest, A Journey of Significant Vision

Preface

"Ladies Can We Talk" initially started out as a personal journey for me. For years I could not understand why it was; that no matter what project I started it seemed I was always one step short of getting it completed. I never understood why I gave so much love yet, always fell short of receiving back in the same capacity. How was it that words spoken either to or over me impacted my life to the degree that I felt I had no self-esteem? No self- worth?

Secondly, I decided to write because as I haphazardly shuffled through life with no hope or direction, I begin listening to women who had been victimized at some point in their life, and; just like me had given up on themselves. I constantly watched the news over and over again, and saw women, beautiful women, who are now locked behind bars all because of the inward torments that seduced them into making deadly decisions.

In addition to these mishaps I began to hear mothers out in public shouting damnable words to their daughters, and daughters shouting the same at their mothers with no fear or hesitation. My heart ached as I begin to see more and more babies being born into this world to young unwed mothers, who were left alone trying to

PREFACE

financially support them; and, because of the absence of the father, found themselves trapped in the government's system. Oh my God I remember crying out! What is really happening to us?

Finally, in search of truth, I came to the realization that this was much deeper than the tangible misfortunes I faced in my lifetime. Somehow we've fallen prey in the hands of a merciless master, whose only desire is to destroy us and to take us on a path that only leads us further and further away from the true lover of our soul! As I began to focus from where I started to where I am today, it pointed me back to God's original plan He initiated for all mankind, particularly women. How did God see us in the beginning? What did He have in mind when He brought us on the scene? Yes, women we are definitely a part of God's divine plan. No, we're not accidents waiting to happen as some would have us to believe, but we're beautiful, intelligent, nurturing, caring, unique, wonderful inquisitive beings that our father took great pleasure in designing . Each of us unique in our own rights, willing to give love and deserving to be loved. So in writing this book I speak to women of every race, profession, nationality, background, and denomination, and come in agreement with you to bind every curse that has, or ever will be designed, that has been sent to trick and manipulate us from fulfilling every promise of God for our lives, and to walk in our proclaimed destiny.

Valerie D. Jones

ACKNOWLEDGEMENTS

First, I want to thank God for allowing me to live through so many things that could have easily caused me to not only give up on myself, but on life. I want to thank him for taking everything the devil meant for evil against me, and made something wonderful out of my life. I want to thank God for never, ever giving up on me even when I was confused, rebellious, disobedient, and the like. Through God's unconditional love towards me, it is allowing me to finally understand what true love really is.

I want to thank my husband (Albester) for allowing me time to occasionally get away so I could have solitude to put into writing what was on my mind and in my heart. For keeping me laughing some days by doing certain things or saying certain things without realizing just how funny you were when I wanted to just break down and cry. For just being there when our family was faced with gut wrenching circumstances, thank you!

I wish to thank my mother (Vergie Courts-Buxton) rest in peace mama, for training me up in the way that I should go, and true to God's word it has not departed from me. I want to thank you for the times I thought you were too hard on me, but now that I've

ACKNOWLEDGEMENTS

become a woman and have a family of my own, I truly understand the valuable lessons you taught me, one of which was how to trust God no matter what, which you demonstrated not only by your words but by your life you lived in front of me.

I want to thank my father (J.C. Courts) for the long talks on the phone and words of encouragement, and your contagious laugh when I was really feeling sad and missing my mom (Dowe). I thank you daddy for your kind and gentle ways and for being a man of integrity. I learned by watching you how important it is to always keep your word. If there were more men like you, this world would be a much better place to live! Also to my step-mother (Lillian). I thank you for lending an ear, for your phone calls just to say hi and to check on us when my daughter and I was going through a very trying time in our lives, when it seemed like the whole world was on my shoulders. You have no idea what that meant to me.

Thank you to all my children, for being some of the most blessed, loving and giving children any mother would be proud to have. You have always been my biggest fans and I love you dearly. I know God only has great things for you and I know that you will walk in the favor of God all the days of your lives.

To my siblings, what can I say? You have no idea how much I love you. Although we had our ups and downs growing up, it's ok Danny (inside joke), but I wouldn't trade any of you for all the tea in China! We may not always see each other every day, but trust and believe it's not a day that goes by that I'm not praying for you, wishing nothing but the best for you all the days of your lives.

ACKNOWLEDGEMENTS

To all my grandchildren and great-grandchildren, I love you so very, very much. I pray that only God's purpose and plans for your lives will overtake you, and that No weapon that Satan tries to form against you will ever prosper. You all are the delight of my heart!

To my best friend Stephanie D. Chambers (R.I.P), thank you for being a listening ear, a eating buddy, my bible study partner, and most of all a true friend for thirty years. Since you've been gone, I've had to rearrange so many things in my life, because we went through so many things together in this life. One of the things we often talked about was me completing this book, well; that day friend has finally come. My only regret is that I wish you were here to celebrate this day with me, and knowing you, you are, as you're smiling from above and you're looking down on this day. Rest my dear friend I'll see you in the morning!

To my manager Takelia V. Day who gave so unselfishly of your time, knowledge, and information. For taking the time to be a listening ear, and for being that motivation on days I felt so overwhelmed. You helped made this process so much easier with your "Yes You Can" attitude. Thank you for standing with me 100% not letting go until we completed this project. From my heart I say thank you. My prayer for you is that God will continue to pour into you, your family, and your business as you continue to pour into others. I love you sunshine!

Thank you to DQ Spirit Works, LLC for publishing my book. I appreciate all of the information and time you so graciously extended to us in such a spirit of excellence!

ACKNOWLEDGEMENTS

To my extended family and my church family, I love you all. Thank you for all your love, encouragement, prayers, and support.

Special thanks to my Bishop and Co-Pastor, Ted C. and Cheryl A. Willis, for teaching me, praying for me, offering words of wisdom and instruction, and allowing me room and the opportunity to grow in the things of God.

about the author
Valerie D. Jones

Valerie D. Jones third of five children was born in Milwaukee, WI., but grew up in Dayton, OH. She graduated from Roosevelt High School where she majored in Business, and where she was one of the speakers for her graduating class. After graduation she moved to Belzoni, MS. At age 18 she attended a tent revival and gave her life to the Lord. It was at church where she learned how to truly serve out of a sincere heart.

Marrying at 19 years old, and after almost 10 years of a very long abusive and difficult marriage, it ended in divorce. In 1981 she left MS with her two daughters, heart-broken, back-slidden, no direction, no self-esteem and headed back to Ohio by way of Chicago, IL. It was in Chicago where God had a ram in the bush that not only intercepted what Satan had planned for her, but used this elderly woman to remind her just how much God loved her and had so much more for her. Because of the abuse suffered previously, Valerie could not believe that a loving and caring God would allow a person to suffer so many devastating things, so instead of running to God she continued to try to run from God which only left her further wounded and disappointed.

In October 1981 she came to the end of herself, and decided to move back to Dayton. At the request of one of her close friends at the time, she was invited to attend a church service in Blue Ash,

ABOUT THE AUTHOR

KY not realizing that God had a plan to restore her that night which He did, and she has since served God for the past 31 years. Not only is she a minister of the gospel, but God has also anointed her to dance, where she is a part of Chosen Dance Ministry under the leadership of Bishop Ted C. and Pastor Cheryl A. Willis. Valerie wrote her first short story entitled "Quit or Get Stronger" which was published in the book "Free to Fly" written by Ms. Penda James. Valerie's love for God and heart for women who are, and have been abused prompted her to write this book. She is a wife, Motivational Speaker, Entrepreneur, Songwriter, mother of nine beautiful children, twenty-one grandchildren, and two-great-grandchildren. She attended Sinclair Community College taking classes in American Sign Language. Her heart's desire is to see broken women everywhere healed, delivered, and set free, loving themselves and seeing themselves as God sees them, as they walk in their divine purpose ordained by our Heavenly Father.

Introduction

"Ladies Can We Talk" is an eye opener to help women look inwardly and understand that 95% of the things we've faced, fought through, got defeated in, left devastated, were direct hits from the pit of hell. This book will unlock some hidden truths that for most of us until today are still unaware of. It will help bring clarity to you, and the reassurance that you were not a mistake, but that when God created you, He saw a life that was full of purpose and destiny. You will walk through each page of this book knowing that as you read, chains will be broken, and yokes destroyed from you.

One of the things Satan banks on is that you won't read this book through its entirety, but; I trust and pray over you now, that the spirit of the living God will quicken your spirit and put a deep thirst within you, that; not only will you complete it, but you will receive divine revelation from page to page as you begin your journey. Take as much time as you need to get through each page, some chapters, you might find yourself repeating and that's ok, as long as you get the understanding, revelation, and deliverance you need.

INTRODUCTION

As you go through this book be prepared to cry, laugh, and forgive. Cry, because you will discover how you've been deceived, manipulated, and blind-sided. Laugh, because the yokes will be destroyed as you read, and chains that have had you bound for years, will fall off. Forgive, because you will understand that it wasn't the person or people who hurt you, but they were influenced by the demonic masterminding of Satan who was trying to destroy you before you realized who you truly are. It will become clear how he stopped at nothing to try and prevent you from fulfilling your purpose, your destiny.

What I desire most, is after you've read this book, after the chains have been broken and yokes destroyed, after you've began your super natural healing from the inside out, that you will give God all the glory for being set free, and then be about your father's business seeking to help other women who are in great need to be totally set free.

So now that we've gotten the introduction out of the way...............

"LADIES CAN WE TALK"

Chapter 1

Where It All Began

Sitting here polishing my nails, drinking a cold glass of ice tea; as I listen to one more crime that has just been committed against another female. Wow, the more I listen to the news, the more I cringe as I sense the urgency to speak to women of every race, every background, every denomination as to what the father has to say about us...............

How did we get here? How in the world do we find ourselves in such unstable, unhealthy relationships? What has happened that makes us stay with men who have no clue as to what it means to truly love a woman and have no desire to learn? What are we really afraid of? Is this God's will for my life? Is this the way life is suppose to be? Will it ever end? How do I change it? What did I do to deserve this?

So many questions, questions that I have asked at one time or another in my life, and a few that I ask even now. I often wonder what makes a man say they love you; yet, in the next breath treat you as if you're less than the gum that may be stuck to his shoe. I don't know about you ladies; but, it's time we do some true soul searching. Not so much as to point blame because we share a little responsibility in that; but, it's time to look deep within to see what's really going on with us; the queen, the princess, the bride that God destined us to be from creation. Creation, ah yes; what a wonderful place to start. In the beginning, God created! Not man, not you, not the doctor, not evolution but God; and, everything He created, He said it was not only good; but, very good. Just think about it. Someone makes that special pie you love; and you sit down to eat a piece without that scoop of ice cream. They might ask "how does it taste?" You then respond "oh it's good". But honey let them enhance that piece of pie by adding a scoop of your favorite ice cream to go along with it, your response will not only be "it was good, but more of a gut wrenching," it was very good." That's how God saw "**everything**" He made which included you and I. Take another look at the book of Genesis. Look how particular and strategically God put things in place; one at a time. I can imagine him taking the time to see it in his mind, and when it felt perfect, when it felt right, when it satisfied his taste, He spoke it into existence.

Every star He flung in space, the beauty of the moon at night, the sun that takes your breath away either while rising or setting, the beauty of various flowers and plants, and the list goes on and on, but my point is He had to take notice and smile as each part of his creation became more and more beautiful, and more complex than the piece before. How awesome is that? God didn't just haphazardly throw things together; but, He skillfully and carefully made everything we see today. Humm, "everything" nothing left out, nothing broken, nothing overlooked, but everything complete in and of itself. Every creature created was given the ability to duplicate and multiply and produce something more beautiful and more detailed than the one before. So beautiful is the love of our father.

As we revisit the story of creation (Genesis 1:1), we understand that at some point Adam had the honor and the privilege to name every animal ever created, but; I can also imagine as he watched the male and female interact with one another, in his heart he was still in need of someone, and not something. I can only imagine how beautiful the garden may have been; and yet further believe that Adam's desire to have someone that he could laugh with, talk with, become intimate with, have children with, provide for, protect, etc., overshadowed all of that beauty he witnessed in the garden of Eden. He needed to feel complete. I believe not having a "soul mate", (not a one night stand) weighed heavy on his mind, so much so until it got God's attention. Why do I say that? If you ever sit and watch how animals respond to each other it simulates how humans interact with each other. The male and female bond with each other, they're intimate with each other, they produce species after their own kind, the male provide for his family, and they protect their families. So, if God created animals to think, act, and respond in such manner, why wouldn't He do the same and even more for man who was made after his likeness and in his image?

Stay with me women for a moment. Some might be saying right now, what has that got to do with anything? It has a lot to do with everything, because our heavenly father did not allow us; (women), to come on the scene until he had put EVERYTHING in place for us. He didn't allow Adam to even have the desire, or feel the need of companionship until all things were in place for his "queen". Just think about it, the garden was thoroughly furnished with food. There was every tree imaginable he could eat from, there was the sweet aroma of every flower we see today and vines that generate their own fragrance, **not to mention he had access to fresh meat as he desired.**

Our father was so concern about us that there was a dew, or mist, that came up from the ground to keep the whole garden air conditioned (He didn't even want us to sweat). In this place we had peace, joy and happiness. In this place we had no fear. We were able to trust without hesitation and love unconditionally. In this place not only did we have the love of a natural man, but more importantly we had the love of our heavenly father, the one who we communed with and He with us (oh the intimacy of a pure undefiled love).

Lets dig a little deeper. Our father loved us so much until He didn't even want us to get dirty! What do I mean, glad you ask! God made Adam out of the dirt. We know that dirt has a lot of composites in it, most of which we consider to be very unsanitary. None of us would dare take a bag of dirt pour it in a skillet then cook and eat it, why? Because of all the impurities that's in it. God didn't go back and re-create us from the dirt, no; He pulled us from the side of Adam. Not from his head to lead him, and definitely not from his feet to be under him, but from his side. This should tell us something about God. He didn't want us to feel less than, nor inferior to, nor above or ahead of Adam; but, he wanted women to understand that our place was to be right beside our Adam to be respected, cherished, and adored.

God wanted us to understand how important we were to him, so much so, that when he saw Adam he also saw Eve, and esteemed them both very highly! So, ladies it was never the intent of our father for us to become entangled with all of the filth Satan tries to ensnare us with, to make us feel like we have to do ungodly things that pains God and us, just to hold on to a man!

I think this is a good time to interject some things a lot of us don't know. The day God allowed us to come into this world apart from Him, not only were your parents standing over you ooooing and awwwwwing, not only were your guardian angels standing over you in the delivery room, but there were also demons from hell who was sent on assignment to spy and report to Satan that you made your arrival into this world. At that point Satan sent out an all point bulletin throughout the demonic kingdom that you must be destroyed at all cost. He realized that your mere existence would someday be instrumental in coming against and wreaking havoc to his kingdom. He knew that every person God allows to come through the birth canal and remain alive would be one more person who could possibly win someone else for the kingdom of

God, by snatching another soul from hell. So, unlike us he started planning and manipulating from the very onset of our arrival.

Most of us if we were to take a look back over our lives would actually see now, how; Satan was at work manipulating and trying to destroy us at an early age, at least I can. Certain things we did, certain places we went, certain things that were done to us, certain words spoken to and over us, all were devised by Satan to cause us to lose our self esteem, our self worth, our dignity, our integrity, our mind, and in some cases our lives; but, thanks be to God, for some reason you and I are still here and I'll tell you why. It's because of divine intervention. God appointed angels that were, and are still, assigned to you and I to help us carry out God's divine plan for our lives. That's right! You have been divinely and purposed by God to carry out a specific plan in your lifetime. I know it might be hard for some of you to believe, but yes, your mere existence is because the father has need of you.

~ Jewels of Wisdom ~

In order to truly be able to love others, I must learn to love God first, and then learn to love myself. Loving me is not wrong, as a matter of fact, the more I think about it, the more I realize just how much I deserve to be loved! It is only through God's eyes that I see just how much He loves me regardless if others love me or not.

(Scripture reference St. John 3:16)

WHERE IT ALL BEGAN

. My Journal/My Thoughts .

WHERE IT ALL BEGAN

. My Journal/My Thoughts .

Chapter 2

There is a Reason Why I'm Here!

In the previous chapter we saw that it was a part of God's plan to bring us on the scene when He saw fit to do so. Whether you were born 20 years ago, 10 years ago, or even a year ago, it's all about the sovereign timing of God. I don't know about you; but, I've often asked myself "why was I born during the time I was born"? I often wondered why I wasn't born during the time of slavery; or, during the time Jesus walked the earth, and it all goes back to God's timing. Maybe I couldn't have handled the lifestyle or the conditions during those times. Maybe, just maybe my faith would not have been strong enough to have been able to stay committed or focused.

Whatever the reason, God knew, so He in his infinite wisdom, kept me hidden and tucked away until the right time, and the right hour that I call "Now".

Think about this. We were divinely hand-picked by our heavenly father, out of all the billion and billion of women in the world, He picked us- that's enough to make you shout! Yet, few of us have yet to realize just how much we really mean to the father, and because we don't understand, this is how Satan continues to get the upper hand.

So, here we are. Where is here? Here is the place you are at this exact moment in your life. No matter your profession, ethnicity, background, education, or state of mind, here is the place you find yourself at this moment. You might be walking out your destiny, sitting in a state of complexity or confusion but this is where you are, and believe it or not God your heavenly father is right with you in your (here) state.

As I'm beginning to understand more and more, I realize that for some our "here" is very painful for so many women. For some, our "here" consist of loneliness, pain, aggravation, irritation, frustration, desperation, mental, physical, or emotional abuse, and instead of us recognizing or being truthful about our "here", many of us choose to close our eyes and live a life of lies, illusions, and false realities. Today can be the beginning of something new, exciting, and different. **Let me tell you today, you can stop the chameleon syndrome if you would just listen to me, and realize you don't have to be everything to everyone while you yourself, remain unfulfilled, and in need.**

In order to begin to focus on your "here", before we can move a step further, we must all without hesitation answer some of the most feared questions concerning us; which are "why am I really here"? How did I end up in this place during this particular time?

There is a Reason Why I'm Here!

Am I here because of the wrong choices I made, or was I forced here because of maliciousness of others? I can't answer for you but I can certainly answer for myself. My "here" is because the father has need of me. Don't get me wrong the light bulb didn't pop on overnight, no, there were years and years of mental, physical, emotional abuse, betrayals, molestations, rape, rejection, disappointments, failures, abandonment, lies, pain, deaths, all of which were orchestrated by Satan to utterly destroy me. However, because; of the love of my heavenly father what was meant for my bad has turned for my good, simply because I now understand I've been placed in this position to help set the captive (my sisters) free. I'm here to loose the bands of wickedness that Satan has around the necks of the queens and princesses of God. I'm still here so that I can be a blessing to other hurting women. I'm here to stand in the gap. I'm here to wreak havoc in Satan's kingdom, I'm here to win souls for the Kingdom of God!

Sounds like a lot? Guess what, there's even more. That's right, God has so much more for us, more than we can ever think or conceive, but for many of us Satan has tricked us by the things he says to us, and the things he does to us. How do I know? Follow me down memory lane ....

There is a Reason Why I'm Here!

~ Jewels of Wisdom ~

Everything happens in our lives for a reason, some things we might understand going in, while other things are only revealed as we walk them out. Whichever way they may come, know that as long as we stay in the center of God's love nothing or no man can pluck us out of His hand, in case you didn't know the fight has already been won because of Christ! This too shall pass!

THERE IS A REASON WHY I'M HERE!

. My Journal/My Thoughts .

There is a Reason Why I'm Here!

. My Journal/My Thoughts .

Chapter 3

What Did I Do?

This is probably the second question we ask when it seems that all of hell has been unleashed on us. Ladies, we were created to be loved and protected. We are nurturers, affectionate, and givers. God has put something within us that will calm the loudest storm just by our touch, presence or sometimes a warm smile. Although this is a good thing we must beware because sometimes, if not channeled correctly we will find ourselves becoming a one stop shop, constantly giving and never receiving, nor taking the time to get revitalized, or rejuvenated. If not made aware of what is actually happening, we will find ourselves being used, abused, and merely existing as the abusers continue to take advantage of us with no conscience.

One thing I'm beginning to understand is there has to be balance in everything we do. The famous Miles Monroe stated "where purpose is not known, abuse exist", oh how true! The word of God says that the more pain we endure when suffering for the sake of Christ, the more glory in the end. Let's not get this confused. As a matter of fact let me repeat; the more pain, the more adversity, the more test and trials we suffer for "righteousness sake", the more glory we shall receive in the end.

The problem is some of us are not suffering for Christ sake, some of us are suffering because we've bought, chewed, and swallowed the lies Satan has been telling us for years. What are some of the lies? Glad you asked! As we go through this partial list just say ouch if it step on your toes and keep going, that's what I did. For instance what about the lie that says, "If I do what he wants me to do he's not going to leave me." Another lie he likes to whisper to us is, "no one wants you", so we settle down with someone who makes us feel worse about ourselves than we already do. He tells us, "we'll never have anything, or amount to anything", so we go out and get us a sugar daddy or even worse, someone else's spouse which consequently helps destroy their marriage and home.

Another lie he tells us "you can make more money prostituting instead of working honest jobs", in an attempt to keep us from lifting our head up with a clear, clean conscience which in the end causes us not to ever feel good about ourselves. He tells us "we're too fat or too skinny", so we go and have dangerous surgeries performed trying to make this body look more appealing, not really understanding the danger we're putting ourselves in as far as our health. He tells us "we'll look more attractive if we do certain things", so we go and start marking up our bodies with tattoos, breast implants, liposuction, face lifts, botox and the like. He tells us "our hair is too short" so we're wearing weave and lace front wigs, or gluing hair in, or "it's too long" so we cut it down to the scalp. He tells us "the shorter, the tighter, the better", so we go out and buy clothes that should only be worn behind closed doors with our spouses.

Instead of coming to a screeching halt we plummet even further. We go out and buy the fake eye lashes, the push up bras, etc, just some of any, and everything, not realizing that all of this is a bate that Satan has dangled before us, because; we, have no clue of who we really are, nor of our self-worth. Inevitably, as sad as it may be we swallow hook, line and sink, forgetting all about the queen our father created us to be, forgotten what was said about everything He made; and find ourselves opening a door by which Satan steps in with an attempt to launch a deadly blow.

Now, before any of my family of sisters start slamming the book shut, I'm by no means against keeping ourselves together and looking beautiful. Trust me, I'm always looking for latest hairstyles, the latest fashions, the new color for the season, the cutest shoe, and the list goes on, but; although some of us might do it just because we like to, there are so many other of us who do it because we feel we have to, and that's a huge difference!

Few of us, when we found ourselves drifting in the wrong direction, were able to see the light when it came on, and recognizing what was happening, we repented before God. We told Satan to take a flying leap and he did for a season. However, for others of us who feel we've taken too big a bite of Satan's bate now feeling hopeless, allow Satan to lie to us further. Once the door has been open and we don't readily close it by counter acting his lies with what the Word of God says about us, he digs down into his death bag even deeper and tries to now kill us with words.

~ Jewels of Wisdom ~

A broken and a contrite spirit are two ways to get the attention of our father, his word promises that he will in no wise cast us away! All of us has taken a drink of life's bitter waters, but it's ok, because what didn't break you will only make you stronger!

What Did I Do?

. My Journal/My Thoughts .

WHAT DID I DO?

. My Journal/My Thoughts .

Chapter 4

Words, Words, and More Words!
This is What They Called Me

Our culture is based on words. Without words there would be no language and without language we would cease to be. Words are used to communicate, to build up, to encourage, correct or discipline, all of which are a part of God's plan, but what happens when the words spoken to or over us does just the opposite? What if instead of building up they're tearing down and come from those who love us yet are destroying us without realizing it.

My mother, whom I love and miss dearly, would sometimes use words that were not the best choice of words when talking to me growing up as a child. I knew my mother loved me, there was no question about it, but sometimes the words she spoke would hurt, and often time left open wounds which she had no idea was happening. Because I was a child I couldn't understand or comprehend what really was going on. I didn't realize that my spirit had been wounded and that I was in desperate need of divine healing. I went about doing a lot of things to try to make people happy all the time, or at least I tried to. For instance I would buy candy for the kids in my classroom at school, so that I would feel like somebody liked me, and because this area in my heart was never healed, I mistakenly took this as to how "love was suppose to feel". My mindset was "just keep giving Valerie, and everything will be alright"! But how many know that this was a trick straight from the pit of hell! You see the more I gave, the more I was expected to give. Oh the evil spirit of deception!

There were so many days I often wondered why I always felt like I didn't belong, felt like I was born in the wrong time, just always feeling like whatever went wrong somehow it was my fault, so what did I do? I relied on what was familiar to do, what I knew to do and I gave and gave and gave until as time grew on I had nothing left to give, and the enemy used that against me because I found myself feeling like I wasn't good enough, or I didn't deserve any better! Now that I understand and know better, as I look back, my mother gave the best that she knew how to give. She loved the best way she knew how to love. I would venture further to say that she gave what she had received as a child. She was in living color, a product of how her mother had been treated as a child, and the same as her mother's mother, so there you have it, a repetition of generations and generations repeating the same vicious cycle; except with each generation Satan strengthened the words spoken to do more damage than he did the generation before.

Words, Words, and More Words!

Most of us have a violin story. If I might share some of mine it will go like this: My sibling who I love dearly today and hold none of this to his charge was two years older than I. From the time I was five years old until the age of thirteen I believed I was adopted. My sibling told me at a very early age that my parents had been killed in a car accident and nobody wanted me so I had to come live with them. Being so young I knew no better, and because it was repeated to me frequently at some point I truly began to believe it.

In my mind it started to make sense to me as I grew a little older why I didn't look like my other siblings, not knowing at the time that I looked like my paternal grandmother's twin, whereas the rest of my siblings had more features that resembled my mother's side of family. So for me it made sense why I was of a lighter complexion and their skin color a few shades darker. As I stated earlier it was not until age thirteen, that I found out I wasn't adopted at all, but can you see the spirit of confusion trying to operate along with rejection and so many other damnable spirits that were jockeying for position?

Not only did Satan try to sabotage my mind at an early age in such a devastating way but also there were words and actions spoken and done to me by my sibling that caused me to cry and feel unwanted. There were things he would do to frighten me when our parents weren't around and as a result of all this negative behavior, I became fearful, intimidated, inferior, etc., which eventually tore my self-esteem and self-worth down. Needless to say this caused a lot of problems for me as I went through my adolescent, teenage and young adult years.

The sad thing about this was, when I became married I found myself always trying to be the peace maker, and when things went wrong, somehow I felt it was my fault based solely on the things my then husband would say. I tried to be the best mother I could possibly be, but looking back, I'm sure some of the same negative behavior I had grown accustomed to while growing up, was unknowingly passed down by me to my daughters; but, praise be to God my father for his delivering and healing power, and giving me the understanding that I now have power to break this and every generational curse off my daughters so that it will not pass down to my grand-daughters to the third and fourth generations!

When we were young girls we had no idea how all of the negative, degrading words that were spoken to, or over us were deep dark wells that Satan had purposely designed. I did not know how to counter act these words with the Word of God at the time, so those same words taught me how to live a life of being deceived, manipulated, raped (being robbed of all the good things God placed there from time of conception) and controlled. It taught me to do just whatever I was told to do, and deception said as long as I did it-it would eliminate a whole lot of problems that quite frankly, I didn't have strength to deal with. It taught me how to live a life trying to please everybody else, without ever thinking about what I wanted, or better yet needed. I guess you could say I cried many silent tears, but no one could see them. I screamed many silent screams, yet they were only audible within me. So many of us are at this very point in our lives, but don't give up ladies, help is on the way!

When we continue on a daily basis to feel hopeless, we become numb to life and we settle without looking for, or believing things will ever change or get better. We tend to become introverts and the words spoken become more real than what any preacher preach, more real than what we see when we look at ourselves in the mirror, more real than when others compliment or encourage us, we become our own worst enemy. What do I mean by that some of you might ask, let me help you out. **The enemy within, is whatever your mind, conscience, even your heart deems to be true.**

The word of God states that whatsoever a man thinkest in his heart, so is he (Proverbs 3:27). Wow! What a profound statement and full of truth. Because of years and years of emotional, mental, and physical abuse, I became everything except who God said I was. Because of the levels of hopelessness, defeat, and desperation, instead of being deceived, I became the deceiver. In the areas I had been manipulated and abused, I became the manipulator and abuser with words I spoke; and, where I allowed others to control and sway me, I eventually broke gait like a prisoner who had been locked away from society for years, moving through life with no direction and no guidance, sound familiar?

I was a walking accident waiting to happen and had no idea, not even a clue that Satan was masterminding the whole thing trying to kill me; before, I found out who I really was; and, that I was here as a part of God's divine plan. Praise God for truth, and for setting me free!

Satan has from the beginning of time understood the weight of words, and how they can change the very course of one's destiny. In Proverbs 18:21 it tells us that death and life lieth in the power of our tongue. Just as Satan preyed on Eve in the garden, he now prey on women in this 21st century. Not only Eve, but look how he manipulated our first father, Adam, and then in his stupidity, tried to manipulate using words with Jesus when he took him on top of the pinnacle. Remember the scripture Matthew 4:1-11? He said to Jesus "if thou be the son of God", how foolish a statement; but, in his persuasion he hoped to get Jesus to say the wrong thing, to think the wrong thing, at the time he was most vulnerable (after a forty day fast).

Come on ladies, just think about it. How on point are we with our words, actions, or deeds, when we feel like the weight of the world is on our shoulders, or when we have a significant other who has just dropped a bombshell on us. We're vulnerable right? We become totally off focused and confused, therefore; allowing Satan- the enemy to have his way with us, which is to always have a desire to destroy us.

You see, it's like the fisherman who is trying to catch that really big fish. He throws in his bait and line watching and anticipating when to snatch his prey (fish) out of the water at the right moment, at the right time. Once captured what does he do? He takes pictures of himself with his prize possession, he smiles from ear to ear, proud of the fact that he waited ever so patiently to get the exact fish he wanted. So it is with Satan.

He banks on the fact that he has more patience than many of us will ever have. He doesn't mind throwing in the bait and waiting. He'll wait for years upon years, as long as he believes that in the end he will have what he patiently sought after, and once he has it, his goal is to kill you, steal from you, and if possible destroy you. (St. John 10:10)

However, Jesus promised that He came so we would have life, and even more than just life, but an abundant life (St. John 10:10). Abundant means more than enough in every area of our lives always flowing, a surplus!

I pray you are beginning to see and understand that words are very powerful, they are like loaded guns that can make you walk around feeling like you're on top of the world; or can cause serious damage and sometimes death when negative words are spewed from the mouth of those we love. Most, if not all of us, have had someone who we trusted, loved, and shared our deepest intimate secrets with. We have all had someone we thought would be in our life forever. We all, at one time or another, have been hurt tremendously just by words spoken to us by our loved one.

Still not convinced? Okay, what about those famous words "I love you, I'll never leave you, God gave you me, you're the only one for me", yada, yada, yada, but at some point what happened when that same love one, for whatever reason lash out at us and use words like; "you're stupid", "you're dumb", "I hate you", "you make me sick", "get out of my life", "I should have never married

Words, Words, and More Words!

you", "I never wanted you anyway", "it's your fault that I cheat", and No-body else will ever want you. What were your reactions?

How did you feel???? Since some of us won't be honest with ourselves, let me tell you how most of us felt. We got depressed, we couldn't eat, we thought about the situation day and night trying to figure out what we did to make this happen, along with what we could do to fix it. We couldn't sleep, our hair fell out, we became bitter, angry, had suicidal thoughts, got revengeful, slept with them over and over hoping that would fix the problem. We slept around thinking it would make us feel better, tried to drink it away, wouldn't get out of bed, start messing around with his best friend to get back at him, got high on drugs and alcohol, all sorts of things, all because of something that was spoken to us. Now mind you, this person had not laid one hand on us, but the weight of their words went down and pierced our soul and before we could realize what was said was not who we were or created to be, we took on every emotion that went with all those negative words and guess what, another demonic door was opened in our lives.

For some of us these doors led us on paths that, had it not been for God, would have carried us into utter darkness, leaving us with a mind that would have never allowed us to know God, or the love God has towards us, and ultimately Satan would have destroyed us forever. But thanks to God our father, MERCY and GRACE said NO!

~ Jewels of Wisdom ~

Don't allow negative words to get you confused as to who we are, we are wonderfully and fearfully made! The day you graced this world with your presence ALL the angels stood at attention, praising God! Know this, even if you have to say it yourself, square your shoulders, look yourself in the mirror and tell yourself you are beautiful, you are marvelous, and you can never be duplicated! WOW!

WORDS, WORDS, AND MORE WORDS!

. My Journal/My Thoughts .

WORDS, WORDS, AND MORE WORDS!

. My Journal/My Thoughts .

Chapter 5

How Do I Get Up From Here?

Remember earlier we said "here" is wherever you find yourself at this very moment. In order to move forward from this place you must first admit where you are. It really does not matter how you got here, what matters is you don't stay here. Repentance is always a good place to start. Why should you repent? Ladies, the reason we all need to repent is because at some point in our lives, we believed lies about ourselves that were contrary to what God's word has said about us.

Listen, anytime, we put anything above the Word of God, it then becomes a God to us, and when we, whether knowingly or unknowingly, trust in, rely on, and believe in it, instead of what God says, it then becomes truth to us. The bible calls this idolatry. Look at the word idolatry, and what does the first four letters spell? Correct, it spells idol. What is an idol? An idol is something we worship and esteem very highly, and God's word tells us not to put anything above him (Exodus 20:3). As a matter of fact it tells us to love him with all of our mind, soul, and spirit, first. If we were to truly understand and do this, it would keep Satan and a lot of his imps far from us, but as my mother used to say "it's not what you know that hurts you, it's what you don't know" (how true mama)!

So, what is repentance? Repentance is when I become consciously aware of the things I've done or said that displeases God and I become sorrowful in my heart that I've done these things against God's word; and, I want to ask for God's forgiveness, with the sole intent of never doing those things again. It's just that simple! There's no magic or 12 step program, it's just a matter of a sincere heart that wants to turn back to God's original plan for us.

So, for all the ladies who are sincere and ready to go to the next phase, say with me this simple prayer of repentance:

Heavenly father, I come to you today knowing that you are a God who truly loves me and understand me in my "here" state. I ask you to forgive me for listening, receiving, accepting and taking ownership of every lie that has ever been dealt to me on Satan's silver platter. I ask that you wash me with your word and cover me with the blood of Jesus that he sacrificed for me on Calvary, and make me whole from the inside out. I invite the Holy Spirit to come in and lead me into truth based on the word of God. Father, I forgive myself as I also forgive every person who has hurt me in any way whether knowingly, or unknowingly, because today I understand hurting people, only hurt other people. So, I pray that every broken place in their lives will be made whole as the broken and bruised places in my life are being healed and restored. Now father, I thank you for hearing my cry, and for wiping every tear from my eye. I thank you father for setting me free, and restoring the broken places in my life, for removing every frown and replacing it with a smile, for giving me peace in the midst of every storm. Thank you father for loving me in the mighty name of Jesus I pray!

~ Jewels of Wisdom ~

Today is a brand new day, the whole world is a door that's just waiting for you to turn the knob and walk on through. Your today is unlike any other. It's been predestined for you, only you! You can paint it any color, you can write your own song, for today you are walking out your destiny!

How Do I Get Up From Here?

. My Journal/My Thoughts .

How Do I Get Up From Here?

. My Journal/My Thoughts .

Chapter 6

What's Next ??

Whew! Now don't you feel better? As you prayed, did you feel the spiritual chains of the enemy falling off? Did you feel the yoke being broken off your neck? Did you feel the baggage you've carried for years being supernaturally detached from you? Did you feel that frown turning into a smile? In other words you are FREE! That's right, it's just that simple! You can dance now because your father has given you beauty for ashes, and his joy and peace for all the sorrow that once held you bound.

Now that you've taken the most important step, you are now ready to move forward. Don't worry, you can move as slow as you need to because you want this second time around in God's personal garden to remain in you throughout eternity. The next most important thing you must do is to acknowledge who He is. What I mean by that is, you must understand that whether married or single, God is your first husband (Isaiah 54:5). Jesus demonstrates and equates his body of believers as the bride of Christ (Ephesians 5:22-33).

Most of us have read, or heard, over and over how Christ loves his bride (the church), how He provides for his bride, how He protects and comforts his bride, how He's jealous over his bride. We see how He cleanses and washes his bride with the word. How he gives his bride good things, how he's faithful, how he shows his bride mercy and grace, how He forgives his bride, how He cleaves to his bride, how He wants only good for his bride, he's patient and kind to her, and the ultimate sacrifice He made for his bride is that He died for her on Calvary's hill, even while we were yet caught up and doing our own thing! (Romans 5:8) Now tell me of any man you know who has all of these qualities working at the same time, ladies, I'll treat you out to dinner!

I know some of us still might be trying to understand, but Jesus gave us an example using the church, to show us how we are to be treated. Now don't get me wrong, I have enough sense to know that we all are going through our own personal makeover men and women alike, and because of our sinful nature some things just simply take time but my question to you is " looking at where you are right now, do you see ANY of these qualities operating on a consistent basis in those with whom you are in a relationship with?" It's gut check time ladies, and keep it real because ultimately it's between you and God.

In 1st Corinthians 13:4-7 it tells us what love is and what it's not. Remember, we have to go back to our point of origin, God's word. God never changed the game plan, man did in the middle of the game, and we fell for it asking no questions. We must retract some misquoted, misguided findings, then began to make declarations that line up with what God's word says about us. For instance Psalm 139:14. Says that we are fearfully and wonderfully made. Do the math my sister, he took time in making us, we are unique in and of ourselves, no duplication, no junk, but beautiful women who are intelligent enough to become who God created us to be, gentle enough to wipe away the tears of those hurting, yet smart enough to recognize that we can do absolutely nothing without him.

Once we truly understand that God has never made any junk, that He loves us unconditionally, we will then begin to understand that we have access to the one who created us and loves us, anytime we need him, and know this deep inside. He is there to listen every single time, to every single word we have to say, no matter the time or whenever we call his name, and He will stay there for as long as we need to talk! Isn't that exciting?

Our first husband wants to establish and build a relationship with us, oh how He longs for it. As we learn how to acknowledge him in everything we do, in every decision we make, as we learn to go to him for everything and delight ourselves in him, it then becomes his pleasure to give us the desires of our heart. Ladies, please get that! Our father will give us the desires of our heart as we delight in him and acknowledge him in all of our ways Psalm 37:4. What does that mean? It means we don't have to get things the wrong way whether it's by manipulating, using our bodies, using flattery eyes, or being enticing, no! We can be clean, upstanding and just ask the lover of our very souls and He will meet every need we have according to his riches in glory. Isn't that good news!

The third thing our father wants us to know is that He has given us power to obtain wealth (Deuteronomy 8:18). Yes, it's true. I know there were a lot of wrong words spoken over and to you; but, the lover of your soul says you can be wealthy. What is wealth? Wealth means we are blessed in every area of our lives. Nothing is lacking, nothing is broken. It means we are complete in everything relative to us, our children, our health, our finances etc. Look inside your heart what do you have a passion for? Look at your hands, how can you use them to make your dream become your reality, not only for yourself but the kingdom of God? We are more than conquerors through him who loves us! If we would just only believe and look solely to Him, all things are possible to them who believe according to Matthew 19:26.

Some of you my sisters God has even spoken to you to go back to school; stop resisting and fighting and just do it! It's going to bless you in the end; it will be part of your ticket that will lead you to great wealth. You're not lazy, you're not dumb, that is an illusion, that's what the enemy told you, but the truth of the matter is you can comprehend and you will understand. You do have the ability to succeed, come on ladies I'm rooting for you! Our father wants us to be above only and never beneath Deut.28:13. He wants us to be lenders and not borrowers.

Your father wants you to know that it's more to you than just having babies by men who won't even help you take care of them; you're so much more than that. He wants you to own your own homes, He wants you to drive your own cars, and have your own bank accounts, yes He does! It's more to you than what you see. Ladies you're not that trick, that hoe, that baby's mama drama (as some men refer to females). You're not that booty call, that one night stand, you're not a mistake, NO! You are the daughters of the most high, you are blessed and highly favored, you are the apple of God's eye, you're queens and your daughters are princesses. You are part of a royal family, because of God!

So, what now? You're coming out of the shadows into the forefront, you're pulling up your sleeves and taking back what you have allowed Satan to steal from you, and even the things you've given him on silver platters, even if you have to do it dragging, staggering, crawling, screaming, kicking it's still ok. I decree and declare you're breaking out of the cocoon of this world's system, and blossoming into the beautiful butterfly God destined you to be. If you truly believe this, say this simple prayer with me:

> *Father, I thank you that you are a God of love, mercy, grace and a second, third, fourth and even a fifth chance. That everything I am and ever hope to be, I will be because of who you are, and whose I am. Beginning today right now, I lay my life in your hands. Every plan you have for me, I ask that you help me to walk it out. Father I pray when the enemy tries to form his weapons against me, I will call upon your name and you will raise a standard against him. I thank you Lord for every door you have closed and now the new doors you have opened for me. I thank you that what the enemy meant for my*

What's Next ??

bad you are turning around for my good. I love you, I thank you and I will forever give you praise in Jesus Name Amen!

What's Next ??

. My Journal/My Thoughts .

WHAT'S NEXT ??

. My Journal/My Thoughts .

Chapter 7

Getting Started

Now that we know what our father desires for us, it's time to get to work. Some of us in time past had others to make it happen for us, well, now, you want to make it happen for yourselves. In doing this, you will discover that you will begin to hold your head high, stick your chest out, (not in pride of course), but as a sense of accomplishment as you smile at the world; why, because you have adopted a new attitude!

A good and positive attitude will make all the difference. When you face any challenge, go in knowing, trusting, and believing that somehow things will work out just fine. Even when you run into obstacles, have set-backs why, because you're not going in by yourselves. This time you have the lover of your soul with you and He wants what's best for you. Many of you for years have relied on the Welfare System, but God has so much better for you. Please understand I'm not condemning anyone if this is where you are right now, for there was a time in my life I was a recipient; but, I knew it was not where I was going to stay. So, I thank God that there is something in place for those who really are in need.

However, if you're able to work it's time to get off the couch, turn off the soap operas, brush yourself off, look yourself in the mirror and say "lets get busy". During the time I was in the system I worked two part-time jobs to make ends meet and sometimes it still wasn't enough, but I kept plugging at it. Why, because I could not allow myself to get comfortable in that lifestyle. I had to remind myself that I wanted more for myself and my children, and I was determined to make it happen. I worked for temporary services for years, then started volunteering at the church I attended which I did faithfully for six years-until finally God opened the door where I began receiving a check.

One thing we must understand is that Satan doesn't care about us getting blessed, what he does care about is that we don't maintain the confidence in knowing that we can have what God's word says we can have on a consistent basis, or that we can consistently do what God's word says we can do. So day after day he tries to mastermind a plan that will throw a monkey-wrench in our achievements and accomplishments with the hope of wearing us down (Daniel 7:25), and we end up back where we started. Never under estimate the demonic world that you cannot see, and trust me it's one ever present.

During the time God had graciously allowed me to get back on my feet, I decided to take my children to Florida. After such a long hard struggle with not being able to do certain things, I felt my children and I deserved a week of enjoyment. It was such a

GETTING STARTED

wonderful week. We went shopping, went to Universal Studio, woke up early stayed up late, just having the time of our lives. Driving back home after the trip all I could do was think about the good time we all had. As I returned back to work on Tuesday I was met by my then pastor who was also my employer only to be told that I had to be laid off, and because he had not taken out social security on me while employed, I wasn't able to draw unemployment, food stamps or anything!

You can only imagine the thoughts that traveled through my mind. I still had a mortgage payment along with all the other responsibilities I had raising 5 children. I could have easily gone back on the system, (to what was comfortable) or better yet found a sugar-daddy, but I had resolved that issue a long time ago, and neither was an option for me. Set-backs will either make you quit or they will make you stronger. I guess for me it was the stronger because I was determined that if one door shut God would open another one. So once again I started my quest of going to work for various temporary services until finally landing a job at the county as a temporary employee which turned into a full-time employee, and have been there for nine years.

Why am I saying all of this? I'm saying this because I want to encourage you as you embark in your new found life of freedom in God. As you continue to embrace what true happiness is really all about, you will grow by leaps and bounds. As you begin to find yourselves there is one thing I encourage you to do, and that is to share. We must never forget where God has brought us from, nor the chains He unwrapped from around our necks. He did it for you so that you will be quick to help the next sister who feels hopeless and stuck, and who thinks she has no way out.

~ Jewels of Wisdom ~

Rain or shine, this is my time to be all I can be, because of your love for me! I take nothing for granted count everyday a blessing, for once I was blind but now I can see!

GETTING STARTED

. My Journal/My Thoughts .

GETTING STARTED

. My Journal/My Thoughts .

Chapter 8

Maintaining Your New Found Freedom

As you continue to walk out your destiny you must always remember the way you perceive things is also very important. Remember it's not so much how or what others see, but how and what you, the "visionary," see. It is important that you see as the father see. Based on how you see yourself, you will become your own worst enemy, or your own number 1 fan. Please know there will be days when you will have to encourage yourself. As you're beginning to get your footing, know that everyone will not always be in your corner, and that's ok, because you all have a different destiny, so just be careful when receiving advice especially from those who are negative and have no desire to better themselves. In other words be cautious who you allow in your inner circle. Inner circles or networking is very important. Not only will those ladies be the ones who will give you that extra push you will need, but also might be able to offer you valuable information that will help you as you embark upon your new journey.

Next, it is important to remember that as you walk out your destiny remember your mind will be the battlefield, you know, where the I should will meet the I shouldn't, or the I can will meet the I can't, but know that if God shows it to you, then you must through faith trust him enough to believe that He will not bring you to a point of anything without already seeing the expected end. The provisions will come as you continue to walk by faith, and not by your sight. Most of what you will do, will definitely be a faith walk. Why, because our father wants to get the glory as you are being glorified. Just as you are beginning to smile, know he is smiling right with you, and the fact of the matter is He simply loves you!

A third thing to remember is to ask God for balance and direction. Balance and direction is very important when taking on any new challenge. For a lot of us we go too far of either spectrum, and leave other important things undone. Line your day up with God's plan He has predestined for you through daily prayer and devotion. This is very important. Talk to your heavenly father, ask him to lead and guide you and He will. Remember, now that you are free, you can talk to him and He will direct your paths (Proverbs 3:6). Don't feel that what you've started has to be completed all in one day. Remember you will be embarking on new land, new prospects, and new directions which will cause you to face new devils and definitely present new challenges for the duration of your lives, so it's ok to slow down, and take your time.

The fourth thing you want to remember is you will be forever moving, growing, and changing, it is important to set a pace for yourself. I know I can hear you thinking; You're probably saying how can I find time out for me? Or, does anyone see all the other things I have to do? What about next year, I'm going on vacation when I can break away! Well, this is where we all must learn to use some wisdom. Before you start any new project please take time to count up the cost (St Luke 14:28). This will save you so much time and wasted energy. I think it is even wise to start with a smaller project first, to get your feet wet if you know what I mean. You want to sit down and "on purpose" write down the vision (Habakkak 2:2). After you have mastered this step, then determine what it will cost to complete it, taking time to find sponsors if you need to, or grants if applicable.

Next, you want to list those who will help you arrive at your goal (if God is allowing you to go this way), and plan a meeting with them at a time when you, nor they, feel tired or rushed. Once you get these important details out of the way you then can begin to establish time lines using short and long term goal as markers. Now that you have gotten the visions from your head to paper, you will have need of much patience. I've heard it said more than once in my lifetime that "patience is a virtue" and something I have to fight to have even today.

I don't know about you, but sometimes all I want to do is just "get it done", "keep it moving", "let's get finish without all of the unnecessary drama", …….., but we all know that sometimes it just don't happen like that and Satan will use this as a opportunity to slide in a spirit of unhealthy stress. However, if we pay close attention to the following simple, yet valuable information, it will help us to recognize unhealthy stress when we see it; and, with wisdom be able to leap over this pitfall and keep trucking.

The spirit of stress: All of us at one time or another deal with stress. None of us are exempt, but how we learn to handle stress can ultimately make or break us. Ladies, sometime we feel we have to put on our red and blue superwoman suit, with the big " S" on front and we're off to save the day. Question is while we're saving the day, who is saving US! Stress is a silent killer. It doesn't let you know, "I'm coming", you just look up and it's here. Stress doesn't have to be a bad thing; but, when you don't realize you're stressing out and continue to go full steam ahead, something somewhere is going to break down.

Anything can become a habit, including stress. How many of us right now feel like we just have to <u>fill in the blank.</u> Even though your body is signaling take a nap, or take a short walk, or don't engage in that conversation right now, or don't answer the telephone right now, **BUT** we push right on by that little inner voice. Most of the time when we ignore it, by time we've completed whatever it may have been, we've gotten a headache, we're exhausted, we're short wired, we feel the tightness in our shoulders and neck, we got much attitude, we're looking crazy at everybody else, all because we allowed ourselves to overstep the body's signals when it was telling us, "Warning, Warning, Warning, "danger zone", and now we've opened our beautiful arms and have welcomed **STRESS** to have it's perfect work in us.

Stress was never meant to be a bad thing. For example sometime stress will help you to keep a deadline of a very important task you may have on your job. It helps to remind you so you won't procrastinate. But we're talking about undue stress that can be avoided and alleviated.

Have you ever known anyone who has allowed stress to become a normal habit for them? (I do, it used to be me) Some of us feel like **if we're not stressed than something is wrong**. If we don't feel the presence of stress in our life, we really can't function. Even when there is nothing to stress about, we seem to find something or do something that will produce stress in our lives. Some of us just feel comfortable being stressed, **WHY**? because it has become a way of life for some of us.

God never intended for us to be **STRESSED OUT** ladies! How do I know? Refer back to chapter one. Remember Adam and Eve and the garden? All Eve had to do was to show up. God showed us through creation how He wants us to be treated and how we are to live. In God's initial plan for us nothing should move us from our peace, good health, jovial nature, and just being whole in every sense of the word. So sisters lets learn to drop the unhealthy stress, **GIVE IT BACK**, it doesn't belong to us!

Think about it, when we're unhappy, nobody around us is happy. The nurturing spirit that God has placed in us somehow disappears. For example; think of how we respond when we're stressed and our children come with a question. Or when we're really working with a short wire, think about how we respond when someone disagrees with us. We could go on and on about stress but God wants us to know today that we can live a life free from everything He has not given us, including stress. It's a process, we have to work at letting it go, it's a learned behavior. Now that we understand the damage unhealthy stress can do we no longer have to allow Satan to keep sabotaging our lives with it. It might take some time but be determine you will not live a stressful life.

We see from the natural side what stress can do to us, but lets flip it and take a look scripturally what we can do when we find ourselves tipping the scale between stress and serenity:

> *Proverbs 3:5* tells us: to Trust in the Lord with all thine heart, and lean not to thine own understanding.
>
> *Proverbs 3:6* tells us: In all thy ways acknowledge him and he shall direct thy paths.
>
> *Proverbs 4:7* says: Wisdom is the principal thing, therefore get wisdom; and with all thy getting get understanding.
>
> *Psalms 24:1* says: The earth is the Lord's and the fullness thereof, the world: and they that dwell therein.
>
> *Isaiah 26:3* says: Thou will keep him in perfect peace, whose mind is stayed on thee: because he trusteth in thee.
>
> *Psalm 46:10* says: Be still and know that I am God: I will be exhalted among the heathen I will be exalted in the earth.

Of course there are many, many other scriptures that will keep you in peace and I know that as you continue re-discovering God's way of doing things He will direct you to other truths in his word. The bottom line is this: whether young or old, married or single, stress will in some form be a part of our lives, but we must learn how to bring balance into our lives so that it won't overtake us.

Ok, remember we talked earlier about balance, well, since we're here for a season, God has also given us some natural things we can do to relieve stress from our lives: The following is a list of practical suggestions that can not only relieve stress, but bring balance into our lives so we can more easily deal with other responsibilities we might have. If you put these simple things into practice you will have more days that you will smile instead of frown:

- Put things into perspective. **EVERYTHING IS NOT A PRIORITY**.
- Do what you can today, and leave what you can't do for tomorrow.
- Take some time out for you. Schedule time into your day for a break whether it's taking a walk, reading a book, or just sitting somewhere quietly.
- If you're feeling pressured, take 10 seconds to breathe. Stop, take some deep breaths before you take action or make a decision.
- If you have a huge task, break it down in small pieces and then decide which pieces you will work on today. (Remember Rome wasn't built in a day)

Maintaining Your New Found Freedom

- Know your limitations and what you can achieve.

- Look at the big picture, if it's too much to handle by yourself either break the project down and do little by little, OR ASK FOR HELP!

- Don't put off things you don't want to face, you will feel better once you have completed a difficult task, or made that difficult phone call.

- Do your best and realize everything won't be perfect.

- Leave your job at work.

- Recognize your triggers and hot buttons, and if someone presses one, stop and think before you take action.

- Eat healthy, go to bed early, and exercise regularly.

- Believe in yourself and your abilities even when you don't have anyone to coax you along.

- Buy paper plates, cups, bowls, plastic wear, paper cups, etc, remember sometimes even having to wash a lot of dishes in one setting can become stressful.

- Take long bubble baths, while listening to soft music, if that doesn't work add candles and put a **"DO NOT DISTURB"** sign on your door.

- Realize there is only **ONE** you. What you can't get done today, there is always tomorrow.

- If you have children who are of age, teach them to pitch in. Give them chores that you know they can do, and **ALLOW** them to do it.

- Don't take everything so **SERIOUSLY**. Realize you are going to make mistakes and when you do correct it if possible, and if you can't just try not to repeat it again.

- Take time to change hats. Give yourself at least 20 minutes to cool down, or shut off from whatever had your attention prior to the new task.

- Be **YOURSELF** don't waste time trying to be somebody else. No one can be YOU better than YOU!

- **LISTEN** to your body. If you're tired, rest. If you're sleepy take a power nap, you'll feel so much better.

- Light some candles unplug the phone put on your favorite CD and just go on a date with YOU!

- **TALK MORE AND HOLLER LESS**, it saves you from a lot of unneeded headaches and stress.

- If after you've tried all of the above and nothing seems to work **REFER BACK TO FIRST INSTRUCTION.**

Ladies we could go on and on, but I believe that if you would read and follow these simple guidelines as outlined in this book you will begin to see things as I've learned to see things, "differently". I believe God will open a river of abundance in your life as you commit your life to change and growth. If you will trust and believe, there is nothing that you can't achieve in life with God. Remember there are no gimmicks, no get rich quick schemes and no overnight

Maintaining Your New Found Freedom

fame as you are in pursuit of your place in this world. Destiny has your name written on it, but it will take discipline, perseverance, tenacity, and faith. Know up front that long hours and possibly some sleepless nights will become your best friend, and your only company will be the passion that drives you towards your destiny. But if you continue and don't give up until you've reached your goal, it will be worth every moment of preparation.

If you have earnestly taken this book to heart and really have a desire to walk in purpose, If you now understand that God from the beginning of time had a divine plan for your life, if you can forgive yourself, and those Satan used to try to abort God's plan for your life, if right here today you no longer want to play the blame game, If you dare to take a stand and say I can do all things through Christ who strengthens me, If you without doubt know that you were not a mistake that your life does have purpose, if you can let go of the past , cleave to the present and look to the future, then I simply ask you to bow your head and repeat this prayer with me:

> *Most gracious and merciful father, I come to you right now, acknowledging that you are the center of my joy. I stand in agreement with women everywhere, around the world, that I am wonderfully and fearfully made, and that you have a divine purpose and plan for my life. I now understand that there is a way that seems right to a man, but the end there of leads to destruction.*
>
> *Father I want to thank you for keeping your hand and*

watchful eye over me when I did not know my value or my worth. I thank you because your love for me is true and genuine, and you have promised to never leave or forsake me.

Father I thank you now that every fetter has been broken, every yoke has been destroyed and no weapon that Satan has formed, is forming, or will form will prosper. I thank you that you have made me the head and not the tail, that you have made me above only, and never beneath, and that you have made me to be a lender and not a borrower.

I thank you father that I can run to you and I am safe from the noisome pestilence. I thank you that everywhere I place my feet I shall possess that land and bring glory to you. Father I also pray that when the days and times of testing come that I will reflect back on you and your undying love for me.

Father I also ask that you will forgive me of all my sins, and come into my heart and reign as Lord, and Saviour, of my life. According to Romans 10:9-10 which says that if I would confess with my mouth that Jesus is Lord, and believe in my heart that God raised him from the dead, and that he was buried , and on the third day rose again where He now sits at your right hand that I am saved! So I praise you now for my Salvation. Now that I have accepted you as Lord and Saviour over my life, I ask that you lead me to the house of God you desire me to go that I might hear and, receive your word and apply everything in my life you have for me.

Father, please have your perfect way in me, and I will forever give you all the glory, and all the praise, Amen.

**Now come on ladies, jump up and do your dance, leap for joy! You are Free!   You are Free!
YOU ARE FREEEEEEEEEEE!**

. My Journal/My Thoughts .

. My Journal/My Thoughts .

~ Jewels of Wisdom ~

For your pleasure the following pages are a compilation of more jewels along with real testimonies of three women whom I love dearly. May you be blessed beyond human comprehension what you are able to ask or think, in the Mighty Name of Jesus is my prayer!

The next time the enemy tries to confuse you just know:

▪ No matter what the circumstance or situation might be it never gives him permission to be unfaithful. A Godly man will want to stay faithful to God and you and work it out.

▪ Don't engage in the past. The past is just that. If you're in a relationship where he won't let go of your past, let the relationship go, you can't move forward if you're constantly looking back.

▪ Just as a leopard can't change his spots, neither can a man change his heart without God. News flash: If God can't change him, you certainly cannot so focus on you, and what you need and keep it moving.

▪ Learn to say NO! and mean it. A cute no is like a thief coming and taking from you anytime he feels like it, why? Because he knows you really don't mean it.

▪ Don't be so quick to fall in love. You must be honest with yourself is it love or lust? You will know by the way he talks, the things he does, and the way he does or doesn't respect you.

▪ Don't settle for a relationship that has you crying more than smiling, you're only cheating yourself. You're worth so much more than that.

▪ Don't get in a relationship just because you have children and think it will make it better; know that most of the times it makes it worse. If it's not Godly inspired please leave it alone

MORE JEWELS OF WISDOM

- Become whole before committing to a relationship because 1 whole plus 1 whole equals completion.

- Know that you are unique and not to be compared to another. What it took for her doesn't mean it will take for you.

- Real men don't just say they love you, they will spend a lifetime showing you.

- Quit reliving what you didn't do, and focus more on what you're going to do!

- Sometimes you have to forget what you feel and focus more on what you know is best for you

- Don't set yourself up to believe that a man can solve all of your problems the only person who can truly do that is God.

- If you don't love being around you, it's next to impossible for others to.

- Act like a queen and trust me your king is not far behind you.

- Always remember you are responsible for your happiness, never leave it to another person to do so, he just might become your god!

- Relationships are built on trust, not giving up the milk without him buying the cow.

- If you really want him to respect you, it must start first with you respecting yourself.

MORE JEWELS OF WISDOM

■ Don't be blinded by bliss, real relationships take work, work, and more work.

■ Trust me if he doesn't learn to love God, he can't possibly know how to love you.

■ If you're doing better without him than with him, why would you stick your head back into the lion's den.

■ If your heart says it's time to move on, put on your walking shoes and get to moving. There might not be a second chance.

■ It's better to have little and be in peace, than to have much and be filled with anguish.

■ Don't allow anyone to play Russian Roulette with your heart, it is what it is. Love doesn't hurt.

■ Sometimes you will forget who you are by trying to hold on to someone who has no clue who they are.

■ Anyone can say they're sorry, how do you know they're genuine? They won't do it again.

■ Remember you are not with him because you're his mother, if he doesn't know the difference you might want to reconsider.

■ Love is the greatest gift of all especially when it's a mutual exchange.

■ Don't feel guilty if you're not in a relationship right now, the clock might be ticking but remember you're on God's time.

- Never be afraid to say I'm sorry, but don't allow it to turn into guilt.

- Date yourself, before you decide to bring someone else into your world.

- When you learn to feel comfortable with who you are, then you will have no problem being comfortable with others.

- Live for today, tomorrow is never promised.

- Don't spend much time crying over spilled milk, sometimes the milk has expired you just didn't know it.

- Don't be afraid of what's ahead of you, with God it can only lead to greatness.

- When you can learn to laugh at yourself, it won't hurt so bad when others laugh at you.

- Life if full of valuable lessons, it's up to you to put the right price tags on them.

- The best thing about falling down, is getting back up.

- It's ok to cry, just know it's better to cry tears of joy than tears of sorrow.

- You can have whatsoever you say, not what he say or they say, but what Jesus says.

- Trust is a precious commodity, don't throw yours away on someone who is not worth your time.

- If you say you can, you will. If you say you can't, you won't.

- Be careful what you ask for, you just might get it.

- Don't give to him more than he's willing to give to you.

- If the only place he wants to take you is to the bedroom, run! He is not the one God has for you.

- Everybody plays the fool at one time or another in their lifetime, but don't let it become your lifestyle.

- If he pulls and you push, its call teamwork. But, If you're doing all the pushing and the pulling, it's called change your team member.

- It's ok to put yourself first sometimes, it will help him understand you're both important.

- Don't play tit for tat, you might end up with this and that.

- Love is not blind but sometimes we are, think about it.

- A gullible woman to a man is like a hungry lion on a prowl.

- Stop, look, and listen it will keep you from a head-on collision.

- There is a difference between being cautious and being stuck.

- If you don't have time for yourself, you're spending too much time on others.

MORE JEWELS OF WISDOM

- You have many seeds to plant, decide what you want to grow in your garden.

- Always holding back can handicap you, sometimes you just have to let go and let God.

- Don't think that you talk too much there's someone who loves to hear what you have to say.

- If he can't keep his promise, chances are he won't keep you.

- Don't just give yourself away, when your knight finally comes all your armor will have been tarnished.

- To think like a queen takes time. It may not be what you see right now; but, it's what has already been established in the mind.

- Keep looking up you won't be prone to see all the filth you're stepping over.

- Don't allow anyone to define you, especially the one who has yet to discover who they are.

- If you and he are not talking the same language, then you're really not talking at all.

- Don't follow anyone who has yet to figure out where he's going.

- Enjoy your life, it's the only one you have.

- Beautiful is not just what you are, it's also what you plan to accomplish.

MORE JEWELS OF WISDOM

- There is a reason God gave you two feet, one being to keep you from falling and two being able to meet any challenge with both feet on the ground.

- Never allow anyone to take what you have, rather let it be given to them when you feel the time is right based on God's word.

- Don't put more credence in what others say about you more than you put on what you say about yourself.

- Don't live your life for others, you will find you'll be much happier.

- Love your children they are such a blessing, if you be good to them while they're young they'll be good to you when you're older.

- Children don't remember what they didn't have growing up, but they will remember how much time you spent with them.

- If you want to know what perfect love is, look at your babies.

- Who says you can't have it all? It certainly wasn't God.

- God is willing to give just as much as you're able to receive.

- Know when to pass the baton to a new player, especially if the current player refuses to run.

- There will always be someone who looks better, who thinks quicker, but they still can't beat you at being you.

- Go ahead, laugh, it's just a way of releasing all the stress and pressures of today.

▪ To live in this world without God is like being a ship on turbulent waters with no sail.

▪ Open your heart you will be surprised what has been deposited inside.

Testimonies

"BE ENCOURAGED"

TESTIMONIES

I'm Victorious

Everywhere I look, everything I see, mountains and more mountains that's bigger than me. I could run and hide, but that's not my style, I'd rather stand and fight, knowing it will be worth my while. Who said life was easy, it sure wasn't me, but I'm the first partaker, won't you all agree?

    I win some, I lose some, but that's really ok, one thing is for certain I gain strength when I pray. I fight till I win, that's the name of the game, and if you know Him like I do, I pray you're doing the same. Cry if you must, just don't let it last, the word of God tells me, this too shall pass. So take it from me, hold your head high and smile, know that God has your back, and you're always His child!

Written by: Valerie D. Jones

Biography of Ms. Shalonda Stroud

Shalonda C. Stroud second of five children was born in Belzoni, MS., and grew up in Dayton, OH. She attended Residence Park Elementary School, and later received her diploma from Patterson Co-op High School where she studied Medical Arts. Ms. Stroud has a love for life and family. At an early age she became a single mother raising two daughters while working a full-time job. One of her driving forces was she wanted her daughters to learn early in life that in order to have what you need and want you must work for it.

While working at Covenant House Nursing facility, she met the man she would marry, and to this union two step-children came on board, and later one son between them was born. Ms. Stroud has always been big on family. She loved being a wife, and a mother. However, after 10 years of marriage and helping her then husband complete school, this all came to an unexpected end. Finding herself alone, trying to keep her head above water, while trying to finish college, lead her down a road that nearly cost her sanity, and left her with a million unanswered questions.

After two long years of separation she agreed to divorce, and had to come to grips that life must go on. Divorce doesn't have to be the end of your life unless you allow it to, but it can also be the beginning of something new exciting and refreshing. She started looking to God instead of turning from Him. She sincerely asked him to lead her and to direct her in the things she needed to do to get her out of yester-years disappointments. With that being said, she decided to go back to school to complete what she had started.

In June 2011 she graced the stage of the University of Dayton as she received her Associate Degree in Early Childhood Education, from Sinclair Community College. Not only has she mastered this milestone, but is now more determined than ever to complete her nursing degree and becoming a Pediatric Oncology Nurse which she hopes to accomplish in the near future. To date, Ms. Stroud is the owner and director of "Creative Imaginations Learning Center", where she is following one of her lifetime goals. She desires to open other centers as God leads.

If I would say anything today it would be "To God be the glory for all the things He has done, is doing, and will do in my life". Ms. Stroud is the proud parent of Tanajah and Da'Zha Bell, and Mekhi Stroud.

Testimonies

This Too Shall Pass

Written By: Ms. Shalonda Stroud
R.I.P (My Darling)
September 29, 1977-January 8, 2014

Being a mother of five, a wife, and a full time student can be hard on any woman. I know because, I was a mother of five, a wife, and a full time student but things changed, life changed! You see, I went from having two children at an early age, to becoming a wife at an early age. I went from shouldering full responsibility of raising my own children which were only 16 months apart, to raising my then husband's two children one of which who was still in diapers when he came to live with us, which I will admit, at times was very overwhelming considering I was only 21 years old myself. I became married at age of 22 and we had a son together when I was 27. Many days I thought, "WOW, I truly am responsible for taking into consideration the feelings, time, needs and wants of 6 other people before dealing with my own!"

After struggling for the first five years of marriage while living in a small house with all of these children and trying to make ends meet, my husband and I decided to purchase a nice big home that was comfortable and suitable for all of us. After much conversation about wanting to make our lives more comfortable, my husband who had taken some nursing classes previously, decided to go back to school to become an R.N., while encouraging me to stop working outside the home and stay home full time with the children until he got out of school, and then I were to complete my secondary education.

During this time I truly experienced what it meant to become overwhelmed, frustrated, depressed, hurt, angry, sad, happy, bitter, tired, used, mistreated, unappreciated and every now and then loved, all of which was only a hand full of emotions that I felt during this period in my life. It was as if, because, I was at home now, for some reason my then husband felt like he didn't have to help or assist with much of anything anymore. There was little to no conversation upon days at a time, so distance between us started to creep in.

The day finally came that he received his degree in nursing, we all cheered and was so excited for him as his name was called and he walked across the stage. Soon after, I decided to pick my dreams back up to pursue a degree in education. However, during this time my marriage became shakier even more, as drastic changes erupted in my home. The communication between my husband and I came to a screeching halt, we begin to frown more than we smiled. We argued more than we laughed, it was as if we had become roommates instead of husband and wife.

Day after day as I struggled to make sure everyone and everything was being taken care of to the best of my ability, he walked out. I was a full time student, I had no money, no job, a home that I couldn't afford, a vehicle that needed much work done to it and memories, some good, and some bad that would last forever. I remember thinking to myself "Oh my God are you kidding me after all I've put into this, after all I've sacrificed! This is too hard, I can't do it, how will I be able to finish school? How will I make it,? What about my children!" The more and more I sat pondering, the more angrier and overwhelmed I became, but; now even more determined to push towards my goal. I didn't know how I was going to continue to drive back and forth to school with my vehicle being barely drivable.

Not realizing it at the time but sometimes God is working behind the scene even in the middle of chaos and confusion. One day when my van was on what appeared to be its last leg, I was blessed by a friend who offered me to take over her truck payments which would have taken me only 5 months to pay off. I was so happy and excited! Finally a breath of fresh air, so I thought, the truck I was so proud of caught on fire four months after I received it, not only did it catch on fire but it caught my other vehicle and house on fire as well. I watched my house, vehicles, and belongings go up in flames and on top of the stress and pressure of that my children started acting out! No one, unless you've experienced such devastation, can really ever relate. I cried to myself, "What else could possibly go wrong!"

Living in a hotel for two months with my children and a dog , while trying to stay strong for them, getting them back and forth to school, and still going to school full time, became almost unbearable, inhumane if you will. Don't get me wrong, my family was always there for me, but; the truth of the matter is they could only do but so much even though they did their best to assist in any way they could. Nevertheless, I started working two jobs and managed to take on 20 credit hours that quarter in order to escape the reality that my then husband of 10 years left me basically with nothing. I realize that all marriages don't always work, for whatever reasons, but; how can your spouse just walk away from their family when things begin to look better for them, when in fact the one you married refused to walk out when there was virtually nothing but bills and children, "WOW".

Thank God for grace and mercy and favor because the house was insured and I was blessed to be able to move into temporary housing for a while. During the time I was there I decided to have someone come out and look at my home to see if it was salvageable. Some might not understand, but as I said earlier not all memories were bad while there, and not only did I really like my home so did my children. My intentions if possible were to try to make our lives as normal as possible, because I realized, not only had I been traumatized, but so had they.

To get me started I spoke with friends (or should I say thought they were friends) of mine who had their own business, had done work for other people I knew, to come take a look at my house. Ready for this? I was bamboozled and taken advantage of. Paid big money to get them started, not only didn't they do the work, but left town with my money and I have yet to find them. At this point my time in the rental house was up and there I was again trying to make something happen when there was nothing I could physically see.

For 5 months I moved around from here to there living mostly in my car. My mom tried to get me to stay there with them, but; I think I felt I had to do this on my own, my way. I'm not sure why I felt I had to do this, but I did. I had one of my daughters staying at my mom's house, my second daughter at my sister's house, and my son and I was basically homeless. Even when I asked his father if he would hold on to our son until I could think things through, until I could figure the next move, he refused.

However, true to His word in another dark time in my life God heard my desperate cry, and allowed a friend who opened their door to me, and once again I was able to breathe a light but sigh of gratitude and relief.

Needless to say going through so many trying times one after another I started having anxiety attacks and was hospitalized for a while because in all reality I wasn't dealing with everything I had gone through, and was going through, in such a short time, but once released "super woman" Shalonda was at it again, pushing my body beyond it's ability to perform correctly.

Can it get any worse? Yes it can! Just over a month or so ago I was diagnosed with breast cancer. No, don't feel sorry for me because I know that it will be alright. I see my future and it's looking mighty bright! To say I wasn't frightened, to say I didn't cry, or to say I didn't ask God why me, over and over again would be the biggest lie since the Easter bunny. However, I just recently started chemo-therapy and I'm taking it one step at a time, but guess what, I'm not alone because He is with me. So I won't worry, I won't fear and I won't complain, because all is well!

So ladies as I sit and talk off and on to God throughout my day, I am learning to face everything head on, knowing that He will take care of me. Only I could come to this conclusion. I've had to take a good hard long look and realize I deserve better for myself and my children. All the many things I've gone through these past months, could have happened to someone else but they didn't, they happened to me. But in them, I had to stop focusing so much on me and I had to think about my children if nothing else.

I had to make it for them because if I didn't who would? I had to show my children that no matter what happens in your life you never give up, you never quit.

I don't care what life throws your way, you sometimes have to let it hit you if you can't dodge it, but you learn from that hit and figure out a way to dodge the next hit that may come. I had to show my children that I am not a failure even if life makes me feel as if I failed. I am not a quitter even if life pushed me to the point I wanted to quit. I am strong even when life tries to weaken me. I have purpose even when life seems to take my purpose on earth away. I am me!

Even through all the turmoil, trials and tribulations that seemed to happen to me in matter of months I still am victorious in my situation. I have a roof over my head that I can call home, I have a vehicle that I purchased straight off the lot, my children are happy and healthy, and yes I have that degree I always wanted. In June 2011 I graced the platform as I walked across the stage of the University of Dayton to receive my Associate Degree in Early Childhood Education! Being the first in my immediate family to graduate from college!

Yes, with God's help I did it! Through it all God was right there with me, holding my hand, whispering in my ear "Trust me, you can do this, don't you give up!" I'm so glad that I listened to those soft whispers throughout the day because those very words helped me move mountains when I thought that I was too weak to push a pebble.

If I can say anything to encourage you I will say you can make it! How do I know, because I'm doing it little by little, day by day. Be proud of who you are, who God made you to be. No matter where you are in life, or what might be going on right now, cry out to your heavenly father and He will hear you, and He will answer your cry.

Never let anyone take anything from you, and always know that if God allows it, it's got to bring glory back to him, and He allowed it because He knows our expected end which is nothing but good for you and your children! In other words you will receive double for every trouble the enemy sent your way, what the enemy meant for evil God will turn it around for your good, so SMILE ladies with God's help we can do it!

114

Testimonies

"Where Do I Go"

Round and round and round I go, where will I stop nobody knows. I'm tired of the abuse, the lies and the tricks, being slapped around, beat on like somebody's trick! Being disrespected, and sexually abused, don't look so surprised, it's all on the news. Why all the hurt, why so much pain, sometimes I feel that I'm going insane.

I do all I can and still even more, I've cried and I've cried yet he walked out the door! Never looking back not even a call, I know deep within he doesn't love me at all. Round and round and round I go, where will I stop nobody knows.

My bills all due, my money real short, still he comes in and takes what I hid on the porch. I dare not say anything, my heart pounds so loud, to keep from being insulted I just stare at the clouds.

When I look up and see how beautiful they are, I can't help but wonder how did I get so far? Far away from everything who God said I am, was it his fault or my fault, right now I can't tell.

Was I so desperate to want what I knew I didn't need, that I was willing to jump in knowing that my heart would just bleed.

Right now here today as I cry my way through, I'm desperately seeking one thing Lord, it's you!

Written by: Valerie D. Jones

Biography of Ms. Stephanie D. Johnson-Chambers

Stephanie D. Chambers was born in Colombia TN but raised in Dayton, OH. She attended Edison Elementary School and later Patterson Co-op where she majored in dentistry. At age 12 she gave her life to the Lord, where she was always excited to be doing whatever she could in the house of God. Stephanie has always had a heart for women. While serving as Co-pastor of Higher Dimensions Prophetic Ministries, she was very active in working closely with the director of the women's ministry, serving and ministering to helpless and hopeless women of the ministry, and homeless women who were housed at the Salvation Army. She always had a heart to serve, even if it meant bearing the brunt of the pain and sorrow that sometimes came with such a position. Her heartfelt smile and sincere heart was always one of her greatest assets.

Stephanie's love for life always kept her searching for the next person she could feed, make smile, love on, etc. She never met any strangers, she was always willing to pitch in and do her part, no matter what it was or who it was. Working at the Senior Citizen's Center was one of the ways she was able to continue to give of herself. She wanted nothing in return but to be remembered as the lady with the big smile, and the big heart.

Although she left this earth much too soon, the impact she left in the lives of so many people will forever be remembered.

Stephanie was the proud mother of three beautiful children and two grandchildren whom she loved dearly.

TESTIMONIES

Life after Divorce

Written By: Ms. Stephanie D. Chambers
R.I. P (My Dear Friend)
June 24, 1964- May 13, 2012

I know you're gone my friend, but your life still speaks. Your laughter, your words of wisdom are still so desperately needed. So from your heart to theirs, if you were here this is what you would still say:

When a girl is young, she often dreams about life after leaving home. Usually in mind, she plans to be married, and displays her idea of a wedding with her dolls. She just doesn't stop with the wedding; she also plans for life after, by making children with those dolls, and even talking to her husband that's created in mind while she plays house. Never once does she plan for a divorce because her *Cinderella* dreams are to live "happily ever after."

When a woman walks down that wedding aisle, she is like that little girl with a vision and heart of living "happily ever after." By no means, does the thought of divorce come to mind when she faces her love to express the vows of promise to him. If you would categorize a divorce with dreams, it would be called a "nightmare." I was that little girl with a dream of love and a marriage. My hope was to remain in "till death do us part." After being together with my spouse for nearly 25 years, I knew that my dreams would come true….but something happened.

One day my husband called and told me he was tired of being married, and was ready to end it all. My mind began to focus on all we had together, and I wondered how he could leave me without even trying to save what we had invested so much time in to build? What happened to the love? What happened to the marriage vows that we promised each other and before God to keep? Apparently, all those questions were how I felt about this relationship; not him, He was gone. What would I do without him? How would I live? I depended upon my husband to handle my issues of life. I wasn't ready for this new life. I was content with just how it was, and didn't want any change.

I didn't see anything wrong with my spouse. I was happy and I thought he was happy too. He didn't tell me anything was wrong with me or him concerning our marriage. Well, here I was now, standing all alone. Where was God? I even felt God left me because He allowed this to happen. I couldn't figure out why He left; when He (God) promised to "never leave me nor forsake me!" (Hebrews 13:6)

I felt I gave my life sincerely unto the Lord. I worked hard in the church, and had done it from the heart for so many years. I didn't ask for much, but my family was what I trusted God to keep together. All of this was a "nightmare," and shouldn't have been happening to me! However, as time went on, I began to understand this event would produce something good in my life, and the hand of God was still resting upon my head.

In the beginning of my new life, I knew I was a wife in love, but because of the grief in my heart I found myself in tears; it seemed like almost daily. I was so broken up, until nothing else mattered but my ex-husband. I thought maybe he would feel sorry for me and come back, when he knew of the struggles I was facing with raising our daughter alone. We had three children together, two boys and a girl. The boys had left home, and our daughter was at the age of twelve when this catastrophe occurred. You can imagine the pain that was placed upon her when "daddy" left home. One thing he asked of me was to remain his *friend* after he would leave.

I thought he was true to his word, until the day I placed a call and asked for help in finances. He replied in laughter and said, "You are not my responsibility anymore." I was devastated. I couldn't believe he could become so cold, and didn't care about me anymore. I went around and around in my mind concerning the new place that I stood in life. I tried to make sense of this place, and as long as I did it without God, it was like the children of Israel in the wilderness; living in panic and frustration. I thought maybe if he considered my health issues, he would change his mind and come back to me.

Well, after thinking about his reasons for leaving and my illness was one of them, I quickly removed that from mind. Finally, I began to change my thinking. I stopped focusing on winning him back, and started looking at me. I was still alive and needed to get out of the "quicksand" of my past so I could live again. The first thing I needed to do was REPENT to my Lord for including everyone in my situation except Him. If I had done it sooner than I did, perhaps,

I would have not cried so many tears, and had so many sleepless nights.

Next, I needed to apologize to my daughter for not giving her the attention she needed in the pain she also took on because she lost her dad just like I lost my husband. The main change that took place was the communication between me and God; it had to increase. I had to understand and believe that He was listening when I prayed. I also had to increase my trust in Him. He was a savior, father, friend, but if I allowed Him to be, He would be my HUSBAND too! So, I was ready to accept this new life and its challenges because the King of Kings and Lord of Lords had me in His hands.

It wasn't easy at first. My daughter was angry and demonstrated it many times in school. She got into fights, argued with teachers, and a few times was suspended for actions. She became rebellious with me, and we argued many, many times. I couldn't talk with her dad because he ceased all communication with me. All I could do was text on the cell phone, and wonder if he read what I sent him. I had to approach my "husband in the spirit"....God, and trust Him to direct me with my child on how to handle her.

Today, I am dealing with my LIFE AFTER DIVORCE! I have become more confident of myself and the accomplishments that I am able to obtain. My expectations are high! I deal with God in mind, and listen to the Holy Spirit for the directions shown that He gives concerning my life. I forgave my ex-husband, and am able to face him with a smile and conversation like I do with anyone else. I pray for him and his new spouse that God will help them in life each and every day. My daughter is well, and I never encouraged her to go against her father, but talk to him in order to understand his decisions in life. She graduated from high school top in her class, and is currently attending college majoring in Biology. I'm currently employed and also attending college majoring in Business Information Systems. I believe God to send another love in my life who will be greater because of His promise to me. I open myself to other women who are in this situation as an encouragement that if they trust in God, and put Him in that place of the one who left, EVERYTHING WILL BE ALRIGHT!!

Testimonies

It's Knocking

You would think being a wife and mother was the highlight of my life, until I heard a knock at the door, that made me think twice. I mean, I love being a mother don't get me wrong, and being a wife brought challenges of its own. I thought if I consumed my world with helping everyone else, it would fill the void I had within myself.

But I was so wrong, anything worth having is worth fighting for, and every day I kept hearing that same knock at the door. It was that internal knock that only I could hear, that constant knocking so loud and clear. I must be honest at times I feared, so I chose to ignore it for so many years.

One day when I couldn't take it anymore, I put one foot in front of the other and slowly answered the door. I starred it right in the eyes as it stared back at me, I began to shake and cry uncontrollably. I acknowledged, accepted and embraced what was only meant to be….Yes, destiny found me and accepted all of my flaws and even my insecurities!

So ladies know today, that no matter what anyone say or don't say, you were born with purpose, and destiny. Follow your heart never let go of your dreams!

Written by: Takelia V. Day

Biography of Mrs. Takelia V. Day

Takelia V. Day first of five children was born in Belzoni, MS, and grew up in Dayton, OH. She attended Residence Park Elementary School, and later received her diploma from Patterson Co-op High School where she studied Radio/TV and Marketing. Mrs. Day has always been a hard worker and to date has paid off. Not only does she successfully manage various clients, but is also the CEO-founder of Vonshay Exclusive.

Mrs. Day loves the Lord and enjoys working in the ministry; not just being a lay member, but being an example to other women. Her heart's cry for women everywhere is to let them know you can have everything God has promised you, if you allow him to teach you, and keep a humble heart. She not only wants to experience this way of life for herself, but for women all around the world to know they can have it too!

Her heart's desire is to solely carry out everything God has planned for her to do without hesitation and procrastination. Mrs. Day is married to Tyson Day, Sr., and has two children, Jordan Bernard, and Tyson Day Jr.

If there is a word she would leave to women around the world today, it would be "Don't ever let go of your dreams and never second guess the vision! If God put it in your heart, it can happen and if He showed it to you it will. Never be afraid to step out of the box. Boxes are like comfort zones; when you see that the box you're in allows no more room for growth, it simply means it's time to change the size of your box".

Ladies, simply be blessed and never let go!

Testimonies

Who Says I Can't Have it All?
Written By: Mrs. Takelia V. Day

I remember day dreaming as a kid about my fairytale wedding. I saw my prince charming, being driven by horse in a beautiful chariot and of course me being the greatest mother of all times. I envisioned living in a huge mansion, being married to a wealthy man who would be able to provide me with everything I needed and wanted. Somewhere down the line I would eventually have two children who would have need of nothing, for you see part of the vision I saw had me owning my own business. Yes, in my head I had it all. I thought according to the vision I would be ever so happy, and life was going to be perfect; a skate in the park if you will. I failed to mention that in this vision there would be no disappointments or setbacks. Oh, everything was nice and crystal clear but what I failed to realize in reality was that if I planned to have a life of this magnitude, I was going to have to fight like heck to get it.

Throughout my life I dated here and there and finally said the magic words "I Do" to the man who stole (not actually stole) but; who I gave my heart away to. "I Do", wow did those words have an excitement to them, but; never in a million years was I ready for what "I Do" really meant. What I had to learn rather quickly was that "I Do" meant I will submit, I do meant I will pray for you when I really want to curse you out, I do meant I will stroke your ego even when my ego needed stroking as strongly as his. I do meant I consider your business plans and any other thing that may be of interest to you all while maintaining the vision that God gave me and not losing myself in the process .... I mean GEESH!

Being a wife is nothing anyone can prepare you for. Yes, they can and will offer all the advice in the world prior to marriage but; you will never know exactly what to expect until you are in the position of becoming "Mrs." .... Don't get me wrong marriage is a blessing in and of itself. It's full of love, challenges, joy, compromises, heartaches, pain, laughter, sadness, and the list goes on and on. But what do you do when you have two visionaries in the same house and the visions are opposite of each other, or at the time appear to be?

I love my husband and really enjoyed being his wife, but something was missing. We had fun being with each other and of course we fell out from time to time, but making up was the best part of it all yet there was still something missing. I desired more. I felt so unfulfilled and had no clue at the time as to why. There was a void there and unfortunately my husband couldn't fill it. Both of us worked a full time job in order to survive, and finding the time to spend with each other became more of a challenge and not to mention we both had dreams and aspirations that was screaming to be released from within.

I can remember days just sitting at my desk at work and thinking "Lord, I know it has to be more to my life than this". The harder I worked the more unfulfilled I became at the end of the day. I often wondered, if I felt this way was he feeling this as well? This went on for months, how many know about the torment of the mind? It can truly be a dangerous place when you're not rooted and grounded in God's word as you should be. I remember my mind just being a barrel of questions that I had no answers for. Do you put your dreams on hold or pursue them? I tried putting everything on hold in an attempt to become a better wife, but still felt unfulfilled, and dissatisfied at the end of the day. I felt like I was being torn between what I needed to do, what I wanted to do, and what I was expected to do, something just had to give! There was this inkling down on the inside of me to go for it, but the desire to want and maintain peace in my home stopped me from moving forward. Don't get me wrong my husband never interfered or tried to prevent me from pursuing my dreams, but his lack of enthusiasm for my vision made me second guess the vision God showed me years ago. I remember lying in bed one night thinking and crying about my own ventures that I knew God had birthed into my spirit. As I tossed and turned facing the reality of what I might have to lose in order to accomplish what I wanted was very uncomfortable but God had me just where He wanted me.

Was I being selfish? What if I reached my goal before he reached his? Would he still love me or resent me? Did I really care one way or the other? Don't judge me ladies I'm just being honest whether right or wrong. Those were questions that I needed to answer as swiftly as possible because my visions were now hanging in the balance. I wish I could say that every question I had was answered that night but they were not. Needless to say I went years and years doing the same thing, but stupidly expecting something different.

As I continued to deal with matters at hand, continued to work on my marriage without losing my vision totally, in the midst of not knowing exactly how or when it changed, I began to focus more on raising my children and making my house more of a home. Being a wife and mother brought such a sense of accomplishment within its own rights. My family brought me so much joy and yes sometimes so many tears! And that's keeping it real. God blessed me with two more visionaries in the house. They had the ability to make me smile the times I wanted to break down, and yes, they kept me busy every day, but when everyone was tucked away in bed at night, when the lights were turned off, I still felt unfulfilled.

I believe because I became so active in the lives of my family and trying to make sure they were striving in their own lane being destined for greatness, it took my mind off of feeling like I had failed on my own journey. It's always easy to give advice but I found it very hard to except my own. I tried making everyone else happy and neglected the most important person beside God, ME! Starting to believe that I was created to leave a legacy behind I did some soul searching and came to the conclusion that there was no way I was going to live my life in fear. If I were to drop dead today what would my life consist of? How many lives would I have touched? What did I instill in my own family? Did I really trust God? God showed me a vision for a set time years ago but He didn't show me how I would get there. I was either going to trust God and what He said or miss the divine appointment.

I had to make a decision and stick with it. The word of God teaches us that all things work together for the good of those that love the Lord and are called according to His purpose. If I was going to satisfy this yearning I had to do something and I mean quickly. The sickening feeling was becoming unbearable. However, the Word of God teaches us that faith without works is dead, (in other words believe and then make a move). I began to write down every vision God gave me which began to make my way plain as to what I needed to do next. The door for every event God opened for me I walked through it and found favor with those involved. Not only was I blessed to make enough to put back into my business, but I was also fortunate enough to have over flow to embark on my next adventure. One of the most important components of everything I was blessed to achieve was the fact that my family was instrumental in every intricate part of the events whether big or small. God could not have given me a more supportive family. Not only did they support me but was also able to use their gifts and talents as well. I'm a firm believer that when God opened the doors for me, it also opened the door for my family and the seed of becoming entrepreneurs has been deposited into their spirit as well.

Where am I today? Well, I'm a child of God who is still happily married to the man I married over nine years ago, and are raising two beautiful children who are the apples of my eye for this I give God all the Glory, Honor and Praise! In conjunction with being a wife and mother, I'm finally walking into purpose. I decided to put down fear and pick up faith and I couldn't be happier. The happier I feel, the more rest I get at night. The more rest I get at night, the more energy I have for my family the next day. I now realize God gave me these visions for a reason and things are finally beginning to make sense. These visions are not for me to just sit on them, but to propel me into my appointed destiny. Everything that God has ordained for me has to fulfill itself and day by day things are still unfolding.

God knew before I was formed in my mother's womb what He would have me to do. God spoke me into existence and everything relative to me. This means He put a void in my life not to make me miserable, but for me to find my way back to Him and allow Him to make known to me who He really is. This feeling of unsettledness was destiny chasing after me and when I stopped running it tagged me. God chose me to be a God fearing, successful, married business woman, and a happy mother of two who is not afraid to do what He is asking me to do. Ladies, if God chose me, He also chose you. It doesn't matter who believes in your vision as long as you do. Don't be afraid to take a chance. Stop running from destiny and simply walk through the door. The question is are you willing to trust God even when things are unclear and answer His call in order to have it all?

Testimonies

From the heart of Valerie

Ladies,

May I be the first to congratulate you on completing one of the most blessed books written that will help eradicate years of bondage that has prevented me and you from colliding into our God given destines. I want to thank you for allowing me to cry with you, scream with you, and get angry with you because of the deceptive masterminded plots and schemes devised by the enemy of our soul, mind, heart, and even our bodies. I want to commend you for breaking barriers that just as I, held you captive because we didn't realize who we really are.

Thank you ladies for stepping into that place where excuses are no longer welcomed, pointing fingers are now a thing of the past, and loving you, as much as you love others is NEVER wrong. Thank you for taking the steps necessary to stand back up, putting that beautiful smile back on your face, squaring your shoulders and facing a world that is ready and waiting on the real you.

Know that you have a voice that need to be heard to silence a storm, arms that are strong enough to embrace those who are hurting. Legs strong enough to go that extra mile to help those who have taken a wrong turn in life. A smile to give to those who are weary and wears a frown because she feel trapped and can't see her way out. Two gentle hands to reach down and pull someone up because she has lost her self esteem.

Ladies never forget how important you are. Never forget you can never be duplicated. Always remember no one can be you better than you can be yourself! Live life-to-the fullest, always continue to learn and grow and just soar ladies, JUST SOAR!!!

www.ingramcontent.com/pod-product-compliance
Lightning Source LLC
LaVergne TN
LVHW051840080426
835512LV00018B/2990